BRIDGING THE GOP GAP

—·—

HOW THE REPUBLICAN PARTY CAN WIN OVER AFRICAN AMERICAN VOTERS WITH INCLUSIVITY AND TRUST WITHOUT COMPROMISING VALUES.

PHILIP BLACKETT

PREFACE

"In the end, it is important to remember that we cannot become what we need to be by remaining what we are."
- Max DePree

As you hold this book in your hands, I invite you to embark on a journey of transformation and growth. *Bridging the GOP Gap* is a guidebook infused with faith-based principles, practical wisdom, and real-world experience, meticulously crafted to showcase the path forward for the Republican Party in winning over African American voters without compromising its values. This book is not a political manifesto; however, it is a testament to the power of inclusivity and trust-building, rooted in the firm bedrock of unwavering values and integrity.

The scope of this book extends beyond mere political strategy, delving into the heart of the matter – the formulation of genuine connections between African Americans and the Republican Party, the cultivation of empathy for one another, and the earnest recognition of shared conservative values and community aspirations united as one collective. It offers a comprehensive roadmap for infusing inclusivity, respect, and an unwavering commitment to addressing pertinent issues into the very fabric of the Republican Party's engagement with African American communities.

This book is for those within the Republican Party who are ardently seeking to expand their political reach and to foster a more inclusive and diverse voter base. It stands as a beacon of hope for those who yearn to see a political landscape where every voice is heard, understood, and valued. It is a testament to the unwavering commitment to building a more vigorous, conservative, and compassionate society.

My decision to pen this book was not arbitrary. Growing up in Tennessee as an African American, my family were Democrats. When I voted in my first presidential election in 2004 while in college, I voted Democrat down the line. In 2008, I will be honest with you. There was nothing stopping me from volunteering and doing my part on Election Day to help elect Barack Obama as the first African American President of the United States. In 2012, there was nothing that was going to stop me from re-electing the first African American President of the United States.

However, in 2016, right before the election, something changed. The Democrat Party at that time did not resonate with me the same way as it had in years past. Democrats of 1992, 1996, 2000 seemed a lot more conservative in their viewpoints and worldviews compared to those of 2012 and 2016.

I found myself not identifying as much with the Democratic party platform in 2016, once I was no longer voting primarily to help make history. The Republican party platform admittedly made more sense in how I identified in 2016 than the Democratic party platform. I compromised that year and voted for the Libertarian candidate with Donald Trump as my second choice in that election. I had a strong feeling that the Libertarian candidate would not win that election, yet

I was not disappointed to see Donald Trump surprise the nation when he became President that year.

In 2020, I changed party affiliation and I voted for Donald Trump for President. In 2024, I will back whoever wins the Republican nomination for President and Vice President. When I approach politics, I proceed as a Christian who is Republican-light with a multi-faceted perspective as a lifelong student of theology, business, politics, and economics.

I share all this to highlight that something changed for me between 2012 and 2016. Something looked and felt differently to me between the two main political parties. As I learned after 2016, I was likely not the only African American who felt that way. In fact, you reading this right now may feel the same way and may be seeing what I am seeing, or at least may see it with greater clarity after reading this book.

In 2024, I see a significant opportunity for the Republican Party to increase its voter base among African Americans unlike in years past. If the party takes that opportunity seriously and more aggressively changes its strategy to appeal more to the African American vote, they can make significant headway towards broadening their base with more African American independents, conservatives, and former Democrats.

This book is written to help point the party in the right direction from my humble lens. It was borne out of witnessing the palpable yearning for change, the resounding hope for a more cohesive and inclusive political discourse. Hypothetically stepping into the shoes of those within the Republican Party seeking to understand and engage African American voters, I realized the dearth of accessible strategies and actionable insights that could authentically bridge the gap within the GOP. This realization became the catalyst for my unwavering commitment to craft this comprehensive guide, filled with tangible strategies and hopefully heartfelt wisdom.

To be clear, this book is not solely about the 2024 election. It is about 2024 and beyond. This book is bigger than any one person, personality, or presidential candidate. It is about the future of the party, the platform, and its political future.

The inspiration behind this book stems from the amalgamation of diverse insights, spiritual principles, and the guidance of esteemed mentors and leaders who have unwaveringly walked the path of inclusivity and empathy. Their wisdom that I have learned from afar has illuminated the way forward, infusing this book with a depth of perspective that transcends the confines of traditional political discourse.

To you, the reader, I express my profound gratitude. Your choice to invest your time and attention in this book is a testament to your unyielding commitment to creating a better, more inclusive society that **breaks the stereotype that all African Americans think, believe, and vote the same**. At the same time, it is helpful to note that if we truly want a more diverse and inclusive society, such diversity and inclusion should not be limited to what someone looks like on the outside but also includes what someone thinks on the inside, even if that person may feel hesitant to share his or her views publicly in fear of how others will react, especially within their own community.

Not all African Americans vote Democrat, just like not all evangelicals are white. We, as an American people, are much more gray than strictly black and white, or extreme liberal vs. extreme conservative, if we only take the time to suspend our prejudices and judgments and actually listen to one another and ask questions beyond the surface to better understand and love one another, even if we disagree on the issues at hand. As you immerse yourself in the pages that follow, may you find the guidance, wisdom, and inspiration you seek to drive meaningful change and foster authentic connections with those who look differently than you yet think similarly as you (and vice versa).

The intended audience for this book is rooted in the politically engaged individuals, candidates and campaign staff within the Republican Party who ardently seek to understand how to effectively engage and attract African American voters. This book is a beacon of hope, infused with faith-based principles, practical strategies, and unwavering values, designed to facilitate the expansion and inclusivity of the Republican Party.

In closing, as you journey through the chapters that lie ahead, let the wisdom within these pages ignite the flames of change within your heart as we move collectively towards a more perfect union than what we have inherited. I implore you to continue reading, for within these words may indeed lie the transformative solutions that you seek.

CONTENTS

1

— · —

OVERCOMING MISCONCEPTIONS: ENGAGING WITH AFRICAN AMERICAN COMMUNITIES

The sun dipped low on the outskirts of Atlanta, casting elongated shadows over the rows of modest homes. Marcus, a middle-aged African American, drove through the neighborhood he knew like the lines on his aging hands. He circled around the block, his eyes catching sight of kids chasing a scuffed-up basketball across uneven driveways. The warm, honeyed light of the evening sun bathed the scene, giving it a tranquil glow.

A respected member of the community, Marcus had carved out a life that balanced his entrepreneurial spirit with his unfaltering faith. His car slowed to a stop outside of a community center where tonight he would hold a meeting, one fraught with more implications than most might understand - not just for his business, but for the aspirations of a community he held so dear.

He meandered into the center, his thoughts circling the issue at hand. The Republican Party sought to garner support within African American communities like his, but struggled against a stubborn current of disbelief and mistrust. The faith that he leaned on in his personal life suggested that all souls deserved redemption, but could a political entity embody such spiritual principles? Could they reimagine their engagement with communities like his as more than just a courtship of votes every two to four years, but as a commitment to invest in, uplift and understand the people behind them for the long term?

Marcus greeted peers with firm handshakes, the murmurs of their conversations weaving into a frenzy of anticipation. They all sensed the gravity of the occasion. As the meeting commenced, he stood, his voice echoing off the walls, instilling a sense of purpose. He spoke of political strategy, yes, but more so of unity, of crossing bridges built on the solid foundation of shared values and respect – a sort of ecumenical embrace of diverse political beliefs.

"Proximity breeds empathy," he mused aloud, a belief that seemed to mirror the teachings of Christ – being among those you wish to serve. To genuinely address their concerns, the Republican Party would have to walk the streets of these neighborhoods, listen to the stories whispered within the walls of homes, and let the pulse of this community dictate the rhythm of their engagement policies. Like a pastor understanding his flock, it wasn't just about delivering sermons but also hearing confessions and visiting those who have been hurt.

As he laid out strategies that spanned from economic incentives to criminal justice reforms, the room's atmosphere thickened with a cautious optimism. It was met with thoughtful nods and indecipherable scribbles on notepads. Marcus, amidst encouraging them to maintain their businesses as a testament to their resilience and well-being, considered Proverbs 15:22: *"Without counsel plans fail, but with many advisers, they succeed."* Perhaps this collective wisdom could guide their course.

Marcus concluded with a reminder that their cause was a marathon, not a sprint. Doors would not open upon the first knock, trust not gained by mere promises. The community would stand by, watching, with discerning eyes; the true measure of intent would emerge in the unguarded moments between the speeches and platforms.

As the group disbanded, lingering in small clusters, Marcus stepped outside, feeling the cool evening air sober his thoughts. How do we, he wondered, bridge the divide between good intentions and tangible outcomes, between political affiliations and human relationships? How does one sculpt a narrative that resonates across such divides, one that amalgamates divine guidance with strategic execution? Would the efforts to heal old wounds and forge new alliances withstand the trials of time and skepticism?

Unraveling the Truth: The Republican Path to African American Hearts and Minds

At its core, the political arena is a landscape of perceptions and realities, and nowhere is this truer than within African American communities when it comes to Republican engagement. Misconceptions have long cast a shadow on the Republican Party's attempts to reach out to this vital segment of the American electorate. Nonetheless, with right action steeped in sincerity, it is not only possible but essential to build new bridges of trust and understanding. This starts, first and foremost, with a comprehensive understanding of the barriers that exist that keep many African Americans disconnected from the Republican Party.

The Bible tells us, "Faith without works is dead," and similarly, outreach devoid of authentic engagement is fruitless. **The Republican Party must not only proclaim its values but exemplify them through proactive involvement with its African American constituencies**. It necessitates listening with an open heart, recognizing the systemic traumas, and striving for policies that manifest the Party's espoused principles of liberty and justice for all.

Delving into the rooted beliefs and attitudes within African American communities reveals a narrative of perceived neglect and insensitivity to their genuine concerns. It is imperative that Republicans address this narrative earnestly. But how? Transformation begins within. The Party must ensure African American voices are not only heard but are influential in crafting the Republican agenda. Visible representation and empowerment of African American leaders within the Party structures is a testament to a commitment to diversity and inclusion.

In setting the stage for a deeper dive into subsequent chapters, it's vital to understand that this book is not a one-off. **The focus is on developing a sustainable, long-term relationship with African American voters—not as a demographic to be won over in election cycles but as invaluable members of the American polity whose well-being is intrinsic to the Party's mission.** The roadmap outlined here is underpinned by respect for religious liberty, commitment to economic prosperity, and an unwavering belief in the Republican Party's core values of family, freedom, and fiscal responsibility.

Charting the Course: Strategies for Genuine Commitment

Employing an instructive voice, let us concentrate on actionable strategies that paint the sincerity of our commitment in unmistaken colors. It begins with promoting economic empowerment through entrepreneurship, self-reliance and job creation, heavily underscored in the Party's agenda, and aligns with the aspirations of many within African American communities. It extends to championing education choices, ensuring every child, regardless of zip code, has access to quality education—a right that aligns with the core American value of opportunity for all.

The path ahead is layered with complexities, but isn't it said in Matthew 19:26, *"With man this is impossible, but with God all things are possible"*? This statement undergirds our mission with the optimism that underpins America's indomitable spirit. The value in genuine, heartfelt engagement, racial reconciliation and the crafting of policies that resonate with the individuals in these communities is immeasurable. With this chapter as our springboard, the subsequent sections will delve into the economy, education, criminal justice reform, and family values, as focal areas where deep connection and understanding can be fostered.

Together, let us embark on a journey of *transformation*, *collaboration*, and *renewal*—a journey that doesn't promise immediate victories but assures the dedication of a Party ready to walk alongside African American communities toward a stronger, more united future. This is not the pursuit of a single election cycle; it is the forging of a legacy that honors the plaque of traditional values upon which the Republican Party stands.

Overcoming Misconceptions: Engaging with African American Communities

To effectively engage with African American communities, the Republican Party must first understand the misconceptions that hinder its efforts to attract more African American voters. **Among the most prevailing misconceptions is the perception that the Republican Party does not genuinely prioritize addressing the concerns of black communities.** This is a significant obstacle in the path towards fostering trust and inclusivity within African American demographics.

To make substantial progress and overcome these misconceptions, it is crucial for the party to take a proactive approach. Actively seeking to engage with African American communities, humbly listening to their concerns, and demonstrating a genuine commitment to understanding and addressing their needs are crucial steps that must be taken.

It's essential to acknowledge that **visible representation of a new generation of African Americans in leadership roles within the party is vital**. This can reassure the community that their voices are being heard and that the party is actively working towards inclusivity. Furthermore, demonstrating sensitivity to racial inequality and social justice issues can help bridge the gap, fostering an environment of understanding and support, even when there is disagreement on how best to resolve such issues.

By coming to terms with these misconceptions, the Republican Party can arrive at a better understanding of the challenges at hand. It can then align its efforts to thoroughly engage with African American communities and begin to establish the trust necessary to shift these misconceptions. Through proactive engagement, genuine commitment, and visible representation, the party can make significant strides towards earning the trust and support of African American voters.

To proactively engage with African American communities and address their concerns, the Republican Party must prioritize listening and understanding. This entails creating opportunities for open dialogue, where the voices of African American individuals are truly heard and valued. **Instead of approaching these communities with preconceived notions, it's essential to approach with an open mind and heart, ready to learn and gain deeper insights**

into the particular challenges and aspirations of African American voters. This involves embracing the principle found in Proverbs 18:13, which states, *"To answer before listening— that is folly and shame."* Understanding the diverse needs and perspectives of African American communities should be the first step in building meaningful relationships and demonstrating the party's commitment to inclusivity and rebuilding trust.

In addition to representation, demonstrating authenticity is crucial in effectively engaging with African American communities. This requires a genuine commitment to addressing systemic issues, racial injustice, and economic disparities. As the Book of Micah 6:8 teaches, *"He has told you, O man, what is good; and what does the Lord require of you but to do justice, and to love kindness, and to walk humbly with your God?"* The Republican Party must not only verbalize their commitment to right historical wrongs but also actively seek to implement policies and initiatives that aim to dismantle barriers as well as to improve the quality of life for African Americans, as well as its other constituents.

Moreover, the party can proactively engage with African American communities by championing educational choice, the sanctity of the family, safer neighborhoods and economic empowerment. By promoting policies and programs that uplift and empower African American individuals and communities, the party can demonstrate a concrete commitment to collaboratively addressing their concerns. This is in alignment with the biblical principle found in Isaiah 1:17, *"Learn to do good; seek justice, correct oppression; bring justice to the fatherless, plead the widow's cause."*

Ultimately, proactively engaging with African American communities involves a continuous commitment to learning, empathy, and action. **As the Republican Party seeks to build bridges and create**

a more inclusive and welcoming environment, it's essential to approach this endeavor with humility, respect, and a genuine desire to effect positive change. By standing in solidarity and addressing the needs of African American voters, the Republican Party can overcome common misconceptions of insensitivity and negligence and build a stronger foundation of trust, respect, and compassion.

Demonstrating Commitment Through Active Listening

To initiate a genuine connection with African American voters, active listening is paramount. This involves more than mere presence at community events or surface-level conversations. **It requires a deep engagement in dialogues, where the underlying concerns and aspirations of the community are not only heard but also fully understood and internalized.** Such interactions honor the Biblical teaching of "listening before speaking" found in James 1:19 (*"Everyone should be quick to listen, slow to speak..."*). By embracing this wisdom, party representatives can build a foundation of trust that is necessary for long-term relationships.

Ensuring Representation in Party Leadership

Visibility matters. Having African American leaders in substantial and influential party roles signals a commitment to diversity and inclusivity. **It's not just about having faces in the crowd, but also having voices in the decision-making rooms.** Voters are keen observers and are more likely to invest their trust in a party that reflects their own image.

Addressing Racial Inequality with Clear Policies

Vague promises will not suffice; the party must articulate clear policies tackling racial inequality. This means having well-defined agendas that tackle systemic issues such as education disparities, family instabilities, economic imbalances, and criminal justice reform. Demonstrating a thorough understanding of these issues—and proposing viable solutions—resonates with a community that seeks positive change.

Authentic Engagement in Community Initiatives

Participation in community initiatives helps to demonstrate a true engagement with voters' priorities. It's about rolling up sleeves and working alongside community members—not just as politicians but as fellow citizens committed to positive change. Such actions reflect the entrepreneurial spirit of stewardship and service, aligning with the Scripture's call to "serve one another humbly in love" as stated in Galatians 5:13.

Confronting and Disavowing Racial Insensitivity

Listen, we all make mistakes, for all of us have fallen short of the glory of God. At times, bridging gaps means acknowledging and correcting past mistakes. This entails a forthright disavowal of racially insensitive comments or undeniably wrong actions by party members and leadership. Such a stance is non-negotiable for a party seeking reconciliation and deeper relationships with African American voters. Resonating with the principle of repentance, the party can actively work towards redemption by promoting dialogue and mutual understanding, as guided by the spirit of Romans 12:18, *"If it is possible, as far as it depends on you, live at peace with everyone."*

Providing Platforms for African American Voices

Empowerment comes with platforms. It is vital for the party to offer not just symbolic but pragmatic ways for African American individuals to voice their concerns, questions and insights. Modern-day iterations of the town hall meetings, online forums, and think tanks with diverse representation ensure that the party is in touch with what resonates with voters on a deeper level. By amplifying these voices, the party embodies the Scriptural encouragement found in Proverbs 31:8-9, which calls for speaking up and judging fairly on behalf of the voiceless.

Fostering Long-Term Commitment and Accountability

Longevity in engagement reflects sincerity. This commitment involves continued accountability post-election cycles, confirming that the enthusiasm to connect and serve extends beyond political victories. As with any profound relationship, trust is built over time and through consistent action. In parallel to Lamentations 3:22-23 that speaks of the Lord's unfailing compassion and mercies being new every morning, similarly, the party's efforts must be renewed daily to reflect its unwavering dedication to African American voters.

In moving forward, it is crucial to remember that overcoming misconceptions and engaging with African American communities is not just a matter of strategy; it is a matter of morality and righteousness. By actively listening to the concerns of African American communities, respecting their experiences, and demonstrating a genuine commitment to addressing their needs, the Republican Party can begin to dismantle the walls of misconception that have hindered its outreach.

The journey ahead will not be without its challenges, but the rewards potentially can be great. The benefits of successfully engaging with African American voters extend far beyond mere political gain; they encompass the fulfillment of striving for inclusivity in our society without the need of a third party to accommodate those who are more moderate and less extreme in their beliefs. Embracing this path will not only lead to a more diverse and robust Republican Party, but it will also foster a democracy that reflects the true spirit of unity and understanding.

2

— • —

FRAMING CORE PRINCIPLES: TAILORING CONSERVATIVE VALUES FOR AFRICAN AMERICAN VOTERS

The sun set quietly over the urban skyline, its golden warmth slipping between the tall structures that were bathed in its dusk hue. On the eighth floor of a high rise, Marcus sat at his desk cluttered with reports and policy briefs, the muffled sounds of the city barely creeping through the thick glass of his office window. He was an architect of ideas, a strategist plotting a course to bridge the chasm between conservative tenets and the lived experiences of African American communities.

Marcus leaned back in his chair, remembering Sundays spent in church pews, where the concept of faith as a small mustard seed could move mountains. This belief was a bedrock for him, not dissimilar to the conservative principles he now advocated for — a cornerstone, he supposed, that could be as transformative politically as it was spiritually. He pondered how these principles of faith could intertwine with economic opportunities to craft a narrative of empowerment.

The office was silent, save for the soft clicking of his keyboard as he typed a draft aimed at communicating these conservative values in a manner that resonated with the hearts and ambitions of his beloved community. He envisioned scenarios where families flourished under the impetus of free-market dynamics, where children surpassed the educational expectations placed upon them because they had access to school choice, and where communities thrived more on self-sufficiency than overdependence on the government for survival.

He took a moment to glance out the window, allowing the bustling sight of people navigating the streets below to pull him out of the confines of his office. In the lives that moved beneath him, he saw entrepreneurs daring to dream, students challenging their boundaries, and hard workers aiming for a piece of the American dream. It grounded his strategy, reminding him that the principles he worked to communicate had to be as tangible as the pavement under those people's feet.

He reflected on his recent conversation with a local business owner, a dialogue that resonated with shared values and the yearning for financial independence through business ownership. Marcus knew firsthand how entrepreneurship could uplift a community, providing not just financial freedom but a sense of pride and self-reliance. The conversation left him with a strengthened resolve to articulate a narrative that spoke to the soul of the entrepreneur, infusing conservative ideology with a spirit of enterprise and innovation.

As action plans and campaign materials stacked around him, Marcus's inner soliloquy continually returned to the binding thread of community empowerment. It became clear that the key to connecting conservative principles with African American voters was in showcasing the practicality of these more traditional values towards helping fulfill their real-life aspirations for a better life for them and for their families.

Yet, the challenge persisted in the how—the craftsmanship of words, the selection of stories that would not only inform but transform. How could he orchestrate a symphony of dialogue that culti-vated belief in policies that some viewed with doubt? He recognized long-standing barriers, but Marcus held on to the belief that there was shared terrain to be found, and it was on this ground that he would build momentum.

Could the principles of faith and free-market economics sing in harmony to a tune that spoke of freedom and prosperity for all cit-izens, regardless of color or creed? Marcus continued his work, his mind a flurry of thoughts, as the city lights ignited one by one, mir-roring the stars above in the slowly darkening sky.

Values Reimagined for Shared Progress

The earnest quest to shape a society where every member can prosper requires the intersection of political acumen and cultural understand-ing. The Republican Party stands at such a crossroads. **Identify-ing conservative principles that can positively impact African American communities doesn't mean a reinvention of core val-ues, but rather a keen and respectful reshaping of these values into a narrative that reflects the unique historical and cultural narratives of African Americans.** To forge this connection, it is essential that the principles of individual liberty, the free market, and limited governmental intervention not only remain intact but are also vividly illustrated as tools for empowering and improving the African American community.

Proverbs 29:18 says, *"Where there is no vision, the people perish."* This ancient wisdom underscores the importance of framing conser-vative values in a way that paints a clear, prospering vision for African Americans in connection to what they ultimately want. Communi-cating these tenets effectively hinges on understanding that the discussions around economic opportunities, educational advancement, and community empowerment aren't theoretical constructs but are, in fact, a lifeline to a demographic that has been systematically underserved.

Conservative ideologies have the potential to resonate profoundly with African American voters when they are framed as pathways to self-sufficiency and prosperity within their communities. The Republican Party must master the language of opportunity and inclusivity, a language that speaks directly to the entrepreneurial spirit and aspirational goals that pulse vigorously in the hearts of many African American citizens. Invoking this entrepreneurial spirit requires assurance that conservative policies are directed towards creating a fertile ground for businesses to flourish, laying the foundation for economic independence, and providing the educational tools necessary for competitive participation in a global economy.

Spiritual wisdom, such as the principles outlined in Micah 6:8, which advocate for acting justly, loving mercy, and walking humbly, can also serve as pivotal reference points in this discourse. Doing so aligns with a faith-driven / Judeo-Christian worldview that many African American voters hold close to their hearts, underscoring a shared value system and building a bridge of common ground upon which to tread towards mutual progress.

Conservative policies presented as mechanisms for community empowerment will not only invoke a motivational narrative but also cement the idea that the Republican Party's vision and that of the African American community are not divergent paths but rather are convergent ones. **It's about creating policies that are effective, yes, but also ensuring that these policies are perceived as reflective of the communal aspirations of African Americans.**

Crafting A Mutual Narrative of Empowerment

In navigating the nuanced landscape of political communication, the Republican Party must understand and articulate how free-market principles bolster the creation of wealth within the African American community. A focus on strong family values, educational opportunities, and entrepreneurship can illustrate a profound alignment with the work ethics and cultural aspirations vested within black communities across the nation. The stage is set, not for an echo of past outreach attempts, but for a revolutionary rethinking on the way these fundamental principles are shared and, most importantly, how they're exemplified in the real world.

As this chapter aims to educate party members on crafting an inclusive message, its spirit lies in the belief that by honoring the heritage, struggles, and dreams of African American individuals, the Republican Party can invigorate its outreach with a noble authenticity. Such authenticity not only earns respect but also weaves a narrative that is embraced rather than imposed—making it clear that conservative values, when tailored thoughtfully, have the power to uplift and transform communities that have been longing for policies that speak directly to their realities.

The Value of Individual Liberties and Personal Empowerment

At the core of conservative values is the belief in **individual liberties** and personal empowerment. These principles align with the desire for **self-determination** and the ability to shape one's own destiny. This resonates deeply within African American communities, where the pursuit of freedom and empowerment has been a longstanding struggle. By framing conservative principles within the context of individual liberties and personal empowerment, the Republican Party can effectively communicate how these values can uplift and support African American individuals and families.

The Power of Free Market Principles and Economic Opportunities

Free market principles, such as entrepreneurship, innovation, and economic freedom, are essential components of conservative ideology. When communicated effectively, these principles can resonate with African American voters by highlighting the potential for economic opportunities, wealth creation, and upward mobility. The Republican Party can tailor its messaging to demonstrate how free market principles can open doors for African American entrepreneurs, small businesses and working professionals, leading to greater economic prosperity and financial independence within their communities.

The Promise of Limited Government Intervention and Community Empowerment

Conservative principles emphasize **limited government intervention** and the **empowerment of local communities**. By highlighting the benefits of less bureaucratic red tape and increased community control, the Republican Party can convey how these principles can directly benefit African American communities. This approach emphasizes the importance of self-reliance, community-driven solutions, and a sense of ownership in shaping the future growth and safety of their neighborhoods and cities.

Integrating Core Principles with Faith-Based Values

Furthermore, integrating core conservative principles with faith-based values can create a powerful connection with African American voters. Many African American communities have a strong foundation in faith, and by aligning conservative principles with spiritual teachings, particularly of the Judeo-Christian nature, the Republican Party can emphasize the values of integrity, compassion, and community service. This integration can demonstrate how conservative policies can align with the deeply held beliefs and traditions of African American voters.

Understanding how to communicate core principles in a way that resonates with African American voters is essential for the Republican Party's strategy to win over this demographic. The message needs to be tailored to effectively communicate how conservative policies can positively impact African American communities. To achieve this, it is crucial to infuse the communication with a sense of reverence, authenticity, warmth, care and respect, drawing a balance between a faith-based perspective and a practical connection between values and desired results.

The Foundation of Trust: A Descriptive Framework

Understanding the historical context is the starting point of our descriptive framework. The Republican Party has a storied past with African American voters, including significant support during the Civil War and Reconstruction era, a legacy owing to figures like Abraham Lincoln and the GOP's initial stance against slavery. However, the contentious times during the Civil Rights Movement, marked by the adoption of the Southern Strategy, and the varying appeal of Black conservatism, have left a complex legacy. This historical backdrop has etched a narrative that continues to shape African American voters' perceptions today.

Historical Context

The narrative of the party's relationship with African American voters cannot be effectively altered without acknowledging this historical context. Understanding how past policies and events have shaped the current landscape creates a foundation upon which new strategies can be built. The GOP's promotion of individual liberties and free market principles often harks back to an era of fundamental shifts in racial policies. Embracing its role in these shifts, and committing to further positive change, is crucial in framing today's conservative values.

Voting Patterns

Next, we analyze voting patterns, revealing a picture of African American loyalty to the Democratic Party that has been relatively unshaken for decades. Socioeconomic factors, identity politics, and the impact of key political leaders have played a part in cementing these patterns. Yet, understanding the intricacies of these trends provides fertile ground for the GOP to recognize areas of opportunity, wherein conservative principles may align with the community's aspirations and lead to political shifts.

Trust and Perceptions

Trust is the linchpin in any relationship, and African American voters' lack of it in the Republican Party is the third component of our framework. This deficit has been influenced by perceptions of the GOP's stance on issues such as racial equality and criminal justice reform, as well as perceptions by some African Americans of Republicans being racist based on recent American political history. Building trust begins with transparent, consistent communication and outreach that demonstrates a long-term commitment to the community, rather than transactional engagement during election cycles.

Case Studies

In the realm of case studies, we find instructive examples of Republican candidates who have made inroads with African American voters. These case studies highlight how tailored messaging, targeted outreach, and genuine community engagement can lead to increased support. Observing the successful strategies and understanding the nuanced approach these candidates took can serve as a beacon for future efforts.

Key Takeaways

Assembling these components together, we chart a nuanced, historical, and evidence-based approach that the Republican Party can employ to engage African American voters effectively. Our key takeaways underscore the necessity of a genuine commitment to these communities, reflected in policies that advance economic opportunity, the role of the family, educational choice, and community empowerment.

Practical Implications

Implementing this framework involves a dynamic process, adapting as social and political landscapes shift. **It requires the GOP to understand historical grievances, respect current perceptions, and genuinely respond to the societal context**. By taking a holistic approach that covers the full spectrum of relationship-building, racial reconciliation, education, and outreach, the GOP can cultivate more favorable conditions for dialogue and support from African American communities.

This descriptive model offers a roadmap for bridging the gaps of the past, informing present strategies, and paving the way for a partnership in the future. The onus is on the Republican Party to apply these insights diligently and consistently if they wish to see a change in African American voting patterns and perceptions. The pathway forward lies not only in policy proposals but also in the manner they are crafted, communicated, and implemented, ensuring they resonate with the lived experiences and aspirations of African American voters.

The Republican Party can also demonstrate its expertise and real-world experience, providing valuable insights and actionable advice rooted in a faith-based worldview. By incorporating references and concepts from the fields of theology, politics, and economics, the party can create a well-rounded narrative that aligns with the multi-faceted nature of the African American community.

In summary, by embracing a faith-driven perspective, offering real-world application, and communicating its core principles in a relatable and respectful manner, the Republican Party can effectively tailor conservative values to win over African American voters.

3

—·—

DIVERSE PERSPECTIVES: NAVIGATING THE INTERSECTING ISSUES OF AFRICAN AMERICAN VOTERS

E ven in the steady hum of the city, Marcus found a semblance of quiet in the early hours of the morning. The sun was just stretching its golden fingers over the horizon of Detroit, an embattled but resilient city. He stood outside the community center he had built from nothing but from dreams and donations, reflecting on the path that brought him there.

The sharp scent of freshly ground coffee wafted from the small kitchen inside the center, mingling with the cool breeze that whispered through the leaves still clinging to the trees. Today, Marcus was to meet with local leaders and activists to discuss a new initiative. They aimed to engage the African American community in the upcoming elections, a community as expansive and varied as the quilts his grandmother used to sew, each patch a different shade, a different texture, and a different story.

He thought of the young people he'd mentored, bright and eager eyes clouded with the shadow of systemic barriers, their aspirations dampened by the drizzle of seemingly perpetual inequity and skepticism. The weight of history bore down on them, an inherited burden of injustices too numerous to name. Yet, their vibrancy and resilience shone through, a testament to the indomitable spirit woven through the generations.

As he turned the key in the lock, the iron tumblers fell into place with a clunk, echoing through the still-hushed streets. Marcus savored the sound, for it resonated with determination. Today's meeting would not just be about voting strategies or campaign slogans. It would dive into the intersection of economics, education, family values —a confluence that shaped lives in ways pundits and politicians often overlooked.

He greeted the staff with nods and small smiles, the kind that strengthen bonds silently. They prepared the meeting space, aligning chairs like soldiers ready for the coming discourse. On the walls hung pictures of leaders past, eyes that urged them on, voices silent but messages clear. The room filled slowly, a mosaic of faces and ages, each bringing with them a slice of the African American experience. In this gathering, there was no singular narrative, but rather a collection of truths speaking to the diverseness of their tales.

Marcus opened the meeting with words that resonated with the wisdom of those who had walked before him and the faith that guided him. "We are here together, not just to address the moment, but to carve a future for those who will come after us," he began, his voice imbued with a gravity that stooped shoulders and bowed heads in attentive reverence.

As they discussed policies and reforms, anecdotes flowed like streams into the river of their collective dreams and aspirations. Marcus knew the road ahead would be twisted and fraught with challenges. But as the room buzzed with ideas and strategies, a silent prayer found its way into his heart, whispering that perhaps this time, they could rend the veil of inequality that had for too long blinded them to their shared humanity.

As Marcus watched the warm interaction, a thought struck him with the force of a revelation, raising a question that cut to the very heart of their endeavor: How could they transform this patchwork of individual experiences into a quilt of collective action, strong enough to cover and protect the dreams of the next generation?

Unearthing the Layers

The landscape of African American political thought and engagement is not a monolith; it is as varied and vibrant as the tapestry of cultures that compose it. **Understanding the nuanced patchwork of concerns, priorities, and experiences within this demographic is paramount to crafting a genuine and effective outreach strategy**. At the heart of this endeavor lies the recognition that African American voters carry with them the weight of intersecting and often conflicting issues — race, economics, education, and morality — that a blanket approach to politics can neither address nor alleviate. This chapter delves into the core of African American diversity of thought, exploring how the Republican Party can extend its principles to resonate profoundly with a community that history has often sidelined.

Venturing into this discussion requires both humility and strategic insight, where the ultimate goal is to bridge the chasms of misunderstanding and mistrust. Recognizing the diversity within the African American demographic is not merely an academic exercise; it is a foundational step towards genuine political engagement. One must acknowledge the varied backgrounds, suffering, triumphs, convictions and dreams to appreciate this group's potential influence on America's political landscape. Shedding preconceptions and the oversimplification of the African American political experience, while also embracing the multifaceted nature of the African American electorate is necessary to cultivate reconciliation, trust and collaboration.

Moving forward involves developing inclusive policy solutions with an acute awareness of how race, economics, education, and criminal justice uniquely and collectively impact African American communities. Such policy must not merely skim the surface but must be born of deep-rooted understanding and a commitment to making lasting, positive change. At the same time, it is imperative to address systemic barriers and historical injustices that linger not just in history books but in the lived realities of many African American citizens. By acknowledging these injustices and actively working to dismantle them, the foundations for a more robust, trust-filled relationship between the African American electorate and the Republican Party can be laid.

Steps to Solidarity: Republican Outreach and the African American Vote

Step 1: Research and Listen

To operate effectively within the political sphere requires a foundation built on knowledge and understanding. Thorough research into the issues African American communities face and earnest listening to the voices articulating these concerns are critical. This means prioritizing first-hand accounts and empirical data over assumptions, and creating spaces for listening that are respectful, inclusive of African Americans from all walks of life, and free from bias.

Step 2: Identify Common Ground

It is within the areas of overlap between Republican values and African American concerns and priorities that fertile ground for dialogue exists. Economic empowerment, educational opportunity, and criminal justice reform, among many others, are territories where mutual benefit can be found and pursued.

Step 3: Tailor Messaging

Communicating with clarity and sensitivity is essential when engaging with African American voters. Tailoring the message requires language and policy propositions that reflect a genuine understanding of this community's unique challenges, or at least a heartfelt desire to better understand, while also aligning with the broader aims of the Republican Party.

Step 4: Engage African American Leaders and Influencers

Building bridges is a journey mapped out by those who know the terrain. Collaboration with African American leaders and voices not only adds authenticity to outreach efforts but also ensures that proposed policies and initiatives are grounded in the community's realities.

Step 5: Be Visible and Accessible

To make an impact, presence and accessibility are non-negotiable. The Republican presence must be constant and considerate, demonstrating through both their words and actions, both publicly and privately, a commitment to be an ally and advocate for African American communities as part of its own.

Every step of this process can be interwoven with spiritual principles, offering a philosophical grounding that invokes both respect and commonality. Motivated by a conviction to uplift and support the pursuit of entrepreneurial dreams and the push towards educational and economic advancement, this chapter serves as a blueprint for action steeped in expertise. It speaks with the wisdom of experience, encouraging perseverance and celebrating the diverse strengths within African American communities.

With professional acumen, to the best of my ability, it outlines tangible strategies for an earnest and impactful engagement with African American voters, integrating insights from diverse fields to foster a comprehensive understanding and a warm, respectful dialogue. The goal is clear: To equip the reader with the tools and perspective necessary to forge a new, more inclusive path forward for the GOP.

Recognizing the Diversity within the African American Demographic

The African American community in the United States is incredibly diverse, encompassing a wide spectrum of experiences, perspectives, and priorities. Within this demographic, there are individuals of different socioeconomic backgrounds, varying levels of education, and distinct opinions on political, economic and social issues. This diversity has a significant impact on political engagement and presents unique challenges and opportunities for political parties, both Democrat and Republican, seeking to connect with more African American voters.

Understanding and acknowledging this diversity is the first step in effectively engaging with the African American community. **It requires a nuanced approach that recognizes the multifaceted nature of this demographic, rather than approaching it with a simplistic, one-size-fits-all strategy.** By recognizing the individuality and diversity within the African American community, the Republican Party can begin to develop inclusive policy solutions and communication strategies that resonate with a broader range of segments within African American voters.

For clarity, it may seem impossible to get 90 - 100% of the African American electorate to vote Republican. **However, at the time of this writing, it is definitely possible for the GOP to build momentum and go from 10-15% of the African American vote to at least 25-30%.** That improvement alone can significantly change the outlook of many elections, as well as political representation, from a local, state and national level, which is why this book can be very helpful towards achieving this aim if the Republican Party honestly shared that same objective.

In order to engage effectively with the African American community, it's essential to appreciate the intersecting issues that impact these individuals. Race, economics, education, and criminal justice are just a few of the complex factors that influence the perspectives and priorities of African American voters. Developing a deep understanding of these intersecting issues is critical in creating more inclusive policies and initiatives that address the specific needs and concerns of diverse African American communities.

Moreover, it's important to recognize the historical and systemic factors that have contributed to the unique experiences of African Americans in the United States. Historical injustices and systemic barriers have had a profound impact on the African American community, shaping their worldviews and influencing their political engagement. By acknowledging and addressing these systemic issues, the Republican Party can demonstrate a genuine commitment to understanding and empowering African American voters.

Policy solutions addressing race within African American communities should acknowledge historical injustices and systemic racism, yet they should focus less on who to blame and more on how to improve the living situations for African Americans. This may involve initiatives aimed at reducing racial disparities and improving quality access in healthcare, housing, and employment. Furthermore, addressing the root causes of racial discrimination through both legislative measures and community outreach can foster trust and inclusivity. This can be done without looking to the government as the Savior for all of African Americans' problems. There is a balance that can be struck between what the government can and should do, as well as what we as individuals, families, places of worship, and communities can do within our own neighborhoods.

Economic policy considerations should focus on bolstering opportunities for upward mobility and wealth creation within African American communities. Encouraging entrepreneurship and growth within small businesses, providing more access to financial literacy earlier to our youth, and investing in vocational and job training programs, in the midst of constant technological change, can work towards bridging the economic and wealth gaps that persist within these communities.

In the realm of **education**, cultivating policy and community-driven solutions that prioritize greater access to quality higher, technical and vocational education for African American youth is crucial. This can involve measures such as increasing support for charter schools in underserved neighborhoods, promoting school choice and youth mentorship programs, and advocating for more parental control in what their children learn in the schools they attend.

Addressing the complex dynamics of **criminal justice** within African American communities necessitates a comprehensive approach. This involves advocating for reforms in policing practices, correctional system rehabilitation programs to prevent recidivism upon release, and fair sentencing policies to help mitigate the disproportionate impact of mass incarceration on African American individuals and families, especially in how it relates to the epidemic of fatherlessness.

These policies must be rooted in a deep sense of reverence and demonstrate expertise derived from real-world experience, all while maintaining a professional and welcoming tone. By infusing these policy solutions with a faith-based perspective, providing tangible results-oriented strategies, and conveying the importance of these initiatives to address the needs of its constituents with persuasiveness, compassion and clarity, the Republican Party can begin to bridge the gap with African American voters.

A Principled Approach to Healing Historical Wounds

In acknowledging the multifaceted nature of African American voters, it is essential to consider the historical struggles that have shaped their experiences, perspectives and worldviews. The legacy of historical discrimination and systemic injustice covers numerous aspects of society, from housing and healthcare to employment and education.

As we pave the way forward, we are called, by **spiritual principles of repentance, righteousness, reconciliation and redemption**, to actively dismantle these barriers and heal the wounds of our fellow brothers and sisters. Scriptures across diverse faiths emphasize the importance of seeking justice and caring for the orphaned, widowed and marginalized; it is incumbent upon us to apply these teachings in redressing historical injustices that continue to affect African American communities today, as many African Americans nationwide may feel without a home in either political party compared to years past.

The **root causes** of disparities must be understood—and addressed—with precision, humility and commitment. For instance, the entrepreneurial spirit within the African American community has often been thwarted by a lack of access to capital, in comparison to other groups of people, representing a hurdle rooted in a history of economic exclusion. By creating policy frameworks that encourage investment in black-owned businesses, we not only stimulate economic growth but also honor the God-given potential within every individual.

By removing systemic barriers, we lay the foundation not for equality of outcome but more for equality of opportunity—a core American value deeply aligned not only with our shared American history with the ideals of a more perfect union as well as achieving "life, liberty and the pursuit of happiness" for everyone, not just a select few, but also with scriptural mandates to "do justice, love kindness, and walk humbly" (Micah 6:8).

Empowerment Through Education

Education stands as a cornerstone for community development and individual success; yet, disparities in educational resources directly correlate with historical segregation and ongoing inequality. An investment in education for African American communities is an invitation to the table of prosperity, allowing the full flourishing of talents and abilities that have been stymied by underfunded schools, the prioritization of unions over parents, and broad disagreement on the right curriculum to teach our children in the 21st century to prepare them for a new world than what we grew up in. Biblical wisdom instructs to *"train up a child in the way he should go, and when he is old, he will not depart from it"* (Proverbs 22:6). To better support the next generation of Americans, including our children, the formulation of policies that provide more education funding, prioritize school choice, and encourage academic excellence above all other classroom agendas is not just mere political strategy—it is a moral imperative.

Criminal Justice Reform as a Path to Restoration

Criminal justice reform is more than policy—it's about preserving respect for the law, healing families, protecting neighborhoods and empowering communities. The disproportionate impact of the criminal justice system on African Americans calls for compassionate yet firm action aligned with principles of restoration. Faith traditions offer visions of reconciliation, repentance of past wrongdoings, and second chances; thus, supporting reforms that address sentencing disparities, promote rehabilitation over punishment, and dismantle the school-to-prison pipeline is a tangible expression of these profound values.

Economic Inclusion as a Love Thy Neighbor Mandate

The cash flow within African American communities is often restrictive, not for lack of work ethic or desire to succeed, but due to systemic barriers in the financial system. Aa a potential parallel, Leviticus 25:35 instructs, *"If your brother becomes poor and cannot maintain himself with you, you shall support him."* Extending a hand up by fostering environments where African American entrepreneurs can thrive is reflective of this scriptural wisdom. This goes beyond small business growth and ownership, for we should proactively prepare, train and upskill the next generation of workers for where the future demand will be, ranging from blue collar trades, STEM careers to artificial intelligence. Formulating policies that enhance financial literacy in our school systems, expand access to credit, and entry into free markets can empower individuals to build wealth that transcends generations—this is the fruition of a mandate for economic inclusion to greater love for our neighbors, regardless of race.

The Integrity of Accessible Healthcare

Seeking to close gaps in healthcare serves not only as an economic issue but a testament to the value of human dignity. It is tragically irrefutable that African American communities often receive lower quality care, leading to accelerated health disparities. This should not be an issue just for the Democratic Party, but it should be an issue for the Republican Party as well, if we believe in loving our neighbors. A commitment to transforming healthcare access emerges from a belief in the sanctity of life—a cornerstone of many faiths—prompting us to ensure that all have the means to lead healthy, whole lives from the womb to the tomb. By realigning healthcare policy and our community care to prioritize more preventive measures, more equal access, and more affordable treatments by competition, rather than government compulsion, we pay homage to the conviction that every person is made in the image of God and thus deserves to be treated as such.

A Solidarity That Bridges Division

Acknowledging the significance of historical injustices is not a political token—it is an act of solidarity and a commitment to creating a better future for African American voters. Acts of solidarity resonate with Biblical calls for unity — "*how good and pleasant it is when God's people live together in unity!*" (Psalm 133:1). This principle requires meaningful dialogue and effective policy, shaped not just by the lessons of history but by the compassion of faith in a God who helps mend broken relationships among His people. When we listen earnestly and respond with care and action, the bond of mutual trust and understanding tightens, knitting the fabric of our communities closer together.

Moving Forward with Resolve and Respect

The task before us is profound, and it requires an unwavering resolve to pursue righteousness and justice in every avenue of policy, as well as encourage such examples to be replicated in our homes with our families and loved ones. It means dedicating ourselves to recognizing and removing the hurdles that African American voters and others face due to lack of trust in the Republican Party stemming from systemic barriers and historical injustices.

At the same time, African American voters often take great social risks to align themselves with a political party other than the Democratic Party, despite what a thorough examination of American political history (going back beyond the relatively recent Civil Rights Movement) can demonstrate if we just simply take the time to learn beyond the loud and repetitive sound bites we hear by talking heads to further their own agendas and narratives. Such voters should feel welcomed by the Republican Party to align with those who share common ground in belief, ideology and worldview, even if they have varying differences in skin color.

By engaging with an entrepreneurial spirit, a drive for educational empowerment, and a commitment to criminal justice reform, among other issues important to the diverse African American population, we can start to right the wrongs of the past and chart a course for a more trusting and inclusive future. This effort must be infused with respect—a recognition of the inherent worth of every individual—and a faithful adherence to the spiritual principles that call us to uplift, support and love one another.

As we continue on this journey to unlock strategies for inclusivity and build trust among African American voters, it is crucial to remind ourselves of the diversity within this demographic and its impact on political engagement. **Understanding the vast array of experiences, perspectives, and priorities held by the African American community is essential to developing meaningful and effective engagement strategies. Developing these inclusive policy solutions demands a deliberate effort to empathetically listen, learn, and respond to the needs of diverse African American communities**. As a friendly reminder, all black people do not think alike. Thus, the spiritual principle of recognizing the inherent value, dignity, and worth of every individual, regardless of their background, should guide our approach. This aligns with the teachings of compassion, love and understanding for the struggles and aspirations of our fellow brothers and sisters. Just as we strive to cultivate such qualities in our personal lives, they should also inform our outreach, engagement, and policy strategies we pursue in the political realm.

Moreover, it is imperative to understand the significance of addressing systemic barriers and historical injustices that have disproportionately impacted African American communities. **By acknowledging and actively seeking to rectify these injustices, reconciling with future generations for the wrongdoings of past (and even long deceased) generations, we can align our efforts with the spiritual principles of justice and righteousness**. This involves committing to the restoration of communities that have been affected by generational sins and iniquities, and it requires the courage and humility to confront the societal structures that have perpetuated these disparities and find ways to collaborate together to bridge the gaps sustained over time towards resolution and redemption towards a brighter day tomorrow.

4

— · —

ACTIVE LISTENING AND BUILDING CONNECTIONS: ENGAGING WITH AFRICAN AMERICAN VOTERS

The sun was just a suggestion on the horizon when Marcus stepped onto his porch, the cool breath of dawn brushing over Silver Hill, a neighborhood cradling both dreams and memories of Atlanta's African American community. With a mug of steaming coffee in his hands, he watched the street slowly light up, pondering the rapport he sought to deepen with this vibrant community of voters.

Inside him, a silent conversation churned like the coffee in his cup. He had witnessed too many politicians speak at communities instead of with them. Marcus believed in an elected official's covenant with the people, a sacred trust that called for the humility of Moses coupled with the resolve of Nehemiah, each tasked with leading and rebuilding, with ears open to the voice of their flock as trusted shepherds.

He recalled a town hall meeting, bright faces fading under harsh lights as their concerns dissolved into the ether, unaddressed. This memory stoked a small fire within him, fuelled by convictions and passages from the gospel that spoke of listening as an act of love. For him, love for his community would manifest in genuinely hearing them, understanding their struggles as if they were his own – the cornerstone of his upcoming campaign.

The clattering of the morning train in the distance punctuated his thoughts, a reminder of the ceaseless march of time and the rhythm of life that waited for no one. He needed to seek out the pulse of the community, to sit down with Mrs. Thompson, who organized the block's annual barbecue, or Mr. Bennett, the unofficial historian of their streets, whose roots ran as deep as the towering oaks lining the sidewalks.

Marcus knew their narratives were the living scripture of his mission, the unwritten parables that could guide his steps. He envisioned a series of kitchen table conversations and church basement gatherings, arenas for dialogue shaped by respect and hunger for truth.

And as the day swung its doors wide open, beckoning the early risers to partake in its endless possibilities, Marcus was resolute in his heart. He would tread these paths not as a harbinger of empty promises but as a student eager to learn from the collective wisdom etched into the very soul of Silver Hill.

He cast a final glance at the sky, now a canvas of orange and pink, as if God Himself was painting hope for a new day. What would it take, he mused, to ensure his commitment to listening was the beacon that guided his community towards a future of their own making?

The Art of Active Engagement: A Path to Genuine Connection

Active listening, the quiet powerhouse of communication, emerges as pivotal for authentically engaging with African American voters. With care and focus, this listening technique transcends mere auditory activity. It embodies concerted attention, harnessing the intricacies of verbal and non-verbal cues to foster genuine understanding and forge stronger communal bonds. It's a practice deeply rooted in respect and empathy, qualities that resonate with spiritual teachings from ancient texts to modern pulpits.

To build bridges to the African American electorate, fostering authentic dialogue is paramount. This entails **not only an exchange of words but also an exchange of humanity – where one seeks to deeply understand the narrative and nuances of another's life experience**. Feedback transforms from a tool of critique to a gift, providing vital insights that enlighten and inform next steps. This active solicitation of perspectives signals a commitment to inclusiveness and responsive leadership, cornerstones of effective governance and community empowerment.

Engagement thrives when partnerships with community leaders and influencers take root. It's the first step in a fruitful journey, establishing invaluable connections and highlighting shared goals that transcend individual ideologies and personal agendas. These alliances act as catalysts for change, enveloped in the warmth of community trust and collective ambition. Emulating the biblical principle of iron sharpening iron, such relationships enhance the capacity for mutual growth and progress.

The heart of this engagement lies in developing empathy. Empathy enables us to step into the shoes of another, to feel the fabric of their challenges, and to share in someone else's aspirations. This is not merely a passive emotional response but a dynamic catalyst that propels one to action. It's a vital ingredient in the recipe for connection, fostering trust, and ensuring that every interaction is steeped in dignity and mutual recognition. The golden rule — treating others as one would like to be treated — underpins the foundational belief that all voices deserve to be heard and valued.

Embracing this path requires a steadfast resolve and unwavering commitment to valuing every story and voice. In this pursuit, one must remember that the fruits of such labor are not immediate but are harvested through consistent effort and sustained presence within the community. What is sown with sincerity and nurtured with diligence will ultimately bloom into a stronger partnership between the Republican Party and African American voters, based on a shared humanity and a joint vision for a promising future for all.

Active listening is a crucial component in engaging with African American voters. It involves more than just hearing words; it requires a genuine effort to understand and empathize with the experiences, concerns, and aspirations of the African American community. This process can be transformative, creating meaningful connections that go beyond surface-level transactions. By actively listening, Republican leaders can demonstrate their commitment to truly understanding the needs of African American voters and building lasting relationships based on trust and mutual respect.

Investing time to humbly seek constructive feedback and earnestly engage in genuine dialogue with African American voters is essential for fostering a sense of togetherness within the Republican Party. It may require a willingness to have tough, uncomfortable conversations in the process of seeking reconciliation, trust and unity. By creating an environment where African American voices are valued and heard, the party can embrace diverse perspectives and address the unique challenges faced by this community.

It's not enough to simply pay lip service to inclusivity — engagement through active listening builds credibility among Republicans and shows a genuine willingness to learn and grow, which is essential for building a strong, united party that represents conservative Americans of all colors.

The value of active listening extends beyond individual interactions—it is also crucial in building relationships with community leaders and influencers within African American communities. By engaging in meaningful conversations and seeking input from these leaders, the party can gain valuable insights and opportunities for collaboration. These individuals often have an intimate understanding of the needs and concerns of their communities, and their insights can be invaluable in shaping inclusive strategies. Such partnerships can demonstrate that the Republican Party is committed to working alongside African American communities to address their concerns and create more positive change for their families than what the Democratic Party can offer as an alternative.

In a business context, seeking feedback and building relationships with community leaders and influencers can be likened to market research and strategic partnerships. Just as businesses seek feedback from their target audience to improve their products and services, political strategists can benefit from feedback from the African American community to tailor their engagement and outreach.

Moreover, just as businesses form strategic partnerships to reach new markets or better understand consumer needs, political leaders can form partnerships with community leaders and influencers to bridge the gap and foster stronger trust and more loyal support.

It is written, *"Rejoice with those who rejoice; mourn with those who mourn"* (Romans 12:15). We must actively apply this Biblical principle in our interactions, demonstrating a deep, heartfelt understanding of the joys and struggles within African American lives and the lives of fellow Republicans. This spiritual grounding can help solidify bonds built not on convenience or strategy, but on shared humanity and mutual respect. Just as faith without works is dead, listening without empathy is empty.

Stepping Into Their Shoes

To cultivate this empathy, we must listen with intent to the stories of African Americans, recognizing the ongoing impact of systemic obstacles not limited to racism but can also include the persistence of the welfare state, the crisis of fatherlessness, and the seemingly lack of care, protection and opportunity in many inner-city neighborhoods. This is not merely about acknowledging history; it's about recognizing the ongoing narrative that continues to shape lives and communities. By focusing on understanding these experiences, Republicans can better articulate policies that resonate with African American voters, because they are grounded in real-life contexts and concerns.

Building Bridges Through Understanding

Embracing empathy calls us to reach out and establish partnerships with influential figures in African American communities, such as church pastors, local business owners, and educators. These leaders serve as the backbone of their communities and hold the trust and respect of their constituents. By engaging with them openly and respectfully, Republicans can gain vital insights into the issues that matter most and forge alliances based on shared values and goals.

Connecting Through Shared Values

African American voters, like all Americans, hold a wide array of values and beliefs, from their faith to their social views. Our mission is to find and emphasize the common ground that exists between many of their values and the principles of the Republican Party. It is indeed possible to advance policies that promote limited government, free markets, respect for law & order, the sanctity of life, economic empowerment, educational choice, and protection of the nuclear family in ways that directly resonate with a significant portion of the African American electorate.

Celebrating Diversity and Unity

Through our collective efforts, and by embracing the diversity of America's fabric, we strive closer to fulfilling our nation's mission of reconciliation and unity. Acknowledging and celebrating African American contributions to our country's history and culture is integral to building a future where every citizen thrives. By weaving these acknowledgments into our public discourse, we affirm that the Republican Party is attuned to the rich tapestry that makes up our nation.

As we seek to engage and connect with more African American voters, let us remember that empathy and understanding are not simply a means to an electoral end every two to four years. They are manifestations of our shared commitment to the enduring principles that define us, not just as Republicans but as compassionate human beings striving for a more perfect union. Through this commitment, we seek not just to win votes, but to win hearts and forge a lasting legacy of inclusivity, trust, and mutual respect.

Proverbs 2:2-5 implores us to *"listen to wisdom and apply understanding to our hearts,"* and this wisdom can extend to active listening as we seek to comprehend the concerns and aspirations of African American communities. Cultivating empathy and understanding to build connections with African American voters is an approach rooted in sincerity and compassion. As we strive to actively listen to and embrace the lived experiences of African Americans, we honor the divine call to *"love our neighbors as ourselves"* (Mark 12:31) towards building more lasting and impactful relationships for the long-term.

5

— · —

THE POWER OF STORYTELLING: CONNECTING THROUGH NARRATIVES

As dawn broke across the sleepy township of Selma, Isaiah, serving as chairman of a local grassroots organization, paced the floor of his modest office, the soles of his shoes gently pressing into the worn carpet. It was the kind of morning where the hum of potential vibrated through the air, a subtle reminder that today, like so many days before it, was ripe with opportunity for change.

Isaiah glanced at the series of photographs on his wall: monochrome images of civil rights marches and rallies, a timetable of history that both inspired and haunted him. It was here, in this town steeped in the legacy of rights won and dreams deferred, that Isaiah planned his most significant initiative yet – a campaign that would bridge political divides and engage the African American community through the power of storytelling.

He thought back to the mentorship programs, the entrepreneurial grants, and the fatherhood initiatives that had helped uplift a generation in the town's black community. These flashes of success weren't just emblematic of what could be achieved through adherence to conservative principles, but also powerful stories that needed to be shared

– narratives illustrating the tenacity and spirit of a people every bit as invested in the American dream as anyone else.

Isaiah's mind drifted to the strategic meetings, where he'd emphasize the importance of relatability over rhetoric. He held firm in his belief that **if the local African American populace could see how their values aligned with those of the conservative movement, the icy barriers erected by years of mistrust might begin to thaw.**

The chirping of a bird outside his window interrupted his reverie. Isaiah watched as it perched on the sill, undaunted and resolute, a mirror to his own determination. The air filled with its sweet song, reminding him of the raw power that lay within simple and pure messages delivered from a genuine place in the heart.

Picking up a brochure from his desk, he ran a finger over the words "Empower, Educate, Elevate." It was these principles he wished to embed within the narratives he crafted, ensuring each story resonated with authenticity and provided a tangible example of how conservative values were already at work in the lives of those he cared about.

As he prepared to present at the upcoming community forum, Isaiah knew he would have to speak to the heart and spirit of his audience, translating policy into personal testimony, similar to that on a Sunday morning. And perhaps it would be one of those unguarded moments, when the room felt the collective pulse of shared experience, where progress would inch forward.

Turning to lock the door behind him, a question lingered in Isaiah's mind, a question that would drive every word spoken and every story told: How can the values that have fortified and driven so many to success also pave the way for new stories of triumph within the African American community?

Unveiling Narratives That Resonate and Transform

In a world where facts, figures and faith often dominate the political conversation, it is the art of storytelling that has the potential to reach even deeper into the hearts and minds of voters. For the Republican Party to meaningfully connect with African American communities, it must master the power of storytelling, an art as ancient as humanity itself. At the core of this chapter lies the understanding that narratives do more than simply entertain—they evoke empathy, establish common ground, and can drive individuals to action.

Within the sphere of public discourse, storytelling has a divine-like capacity to turn abstract principles into palpable experiences that tap into our shared human condition. Scripture itself relies heavily on parables and life stories to impart wisdom and moral lessons, signifying that even the most transcendental truths are best understood through narratives. By engaging with African American voters on this level, Republicans can illuminate how conservative ideologies have practical and positive applications in everyday life.

The impact of effective storytelling on community engagement cannot be overstated. When a political party shares stories that embody their ideals, they are not merely presenting policies; they're narrating a vision of life that could be accessible to every citizen. Learning how to convey such narratives skillfully can bring abstract ideas like fiscal responsibility, safer borders, and entrepreneurship into a relatable and humanized context that resonates with African American electorates.

Community success stories and personal testimonials can serve as testimonials to the virtues of conservative values. Highlighting individuals from African American communities who have thrived under conservative policies not only serves as evidence of these policies' efficacy, but also builds a narrative of hope and possibility. It is here that Republicans can showcase the reality of their commitment to creating opportunities for all, free from the constraints of overarching government intervention.

Moreover, **community initiatives springing from conservative principles** reinforce the party's dedication to social upliftment. When African American voters see on-the-ground projects, such as educational reforms or small business support programs promoting self-reliance and community development, the theoretical tenets of conservatism become more realistic. These narratives of empowerment speak to a shared aspiration for better futures, echoing the entrepreneurial spirit that is often a cornerstone of African American history and culture.

By weaving together anecdotes that highlight the positive impact of conservative principles on individuals and families within African American communities, the party can humanize its platform and make it more relatable. These narratives enable the Republican Party to showcase success stories, community initiatives, and real-world examples of empowerment through conservative values, ultimately conveying a compelling vision for the future that resonates with more African American voters.

The Bridge Evaluation Framework

The effectiveness of initiatives aimed at garnering support from African American voters hinges on a deliberate approach to storytelling and engagement. The Bridge Evaluation Framework is crafted to provide a comprehensive assessment of these efforts. With its structured components, this framework serves as a roadmap to measure the success and foster continuous improvement of outreach strategies.

Objectives and Goals

The establishment of clear objectives and goals is the critical foundation of the framework. **Targets for the Republican Party include enhanced involvement of African American communities in the electoral process, rectification of preconceived notions about the party, and a substantial increase in African American party membership.** Succinctly, the goals encapsulate a vision of a more inclusive and diverse representation within the party ranks, acknowledging the vital role of African American voters in shaping a more holistic Republican future.

Key Performance Indicators

In order to track the success of outreach initiatives, we deploy Key Performance Indicators (KPIs). These metrics include quantifiable data such as the number of new voter registrations, participation rates at elections, favorable shifts in public opinion, and active engagement across social media platforms. KPIs act as the navigational beacons that guide the party's efforts, providing tangible benchmarks to gauge the impact of storytelling in connecting with African American communities.

Implementation Plan

A detailed Implementation Plan is pivotal for actualizing the identified goals. This encompasses the identification of stakeholders, resource allocation, and meticulous timelines. A comprehensive communication strategy, alongside rigorous outreach and grassroots organizing, are instrumental. Additionally, strategic candidate recruitment is vital to ensure representation that resonates with and is representative of African American communities. The plan is the operational blueprint that, when executed effectively, can bridge the gap between the party and African American voters through engaging and relatable storytelling.

Monitoring and Evaluation

To ensure that initiatives are on the right track, a Monitoring and Evaluation system is vital. This includes using a mix of quantitative and qualitative research tools such as surveys, focus groups, and analysis of electoral data. The process also establishes a feedback loop to capture the voices of the community. Monitoring frequencies and scopes are precisely defined to allow for timely insights that can steer the campaign's direction as necessary.

Adjustments and Iterations

The dynamism of political landscapes calls for a framework that accommodates flexibility. By analyzing the results from monitoring and evaluation, the party can make informed adjustments to its initiatives. This iterative process is essential for refinement and enhancement of strategies over time, ensuring they remain effective and relevant to the needs and aspirations of African American voters. It is in this adaptable nature that the framework supports sustainable growth and proficiency in reaching and connecting with the community.

As we move forward, let us remember the words of Proverbs 11:25, *"A generous person will prosper; whoever refreshes others will be refreshed."* Our duty is to refresh the hearts and minds of our fellow citizens through our stories, inspiring hope and planting the seeds of a shared vision for a better future than the Democratic status quo. These narratives must not merely be tales of rhetoric, but rather living testimonies of family empowerment and community transformation through the adoption of conservative values.

Effective storytelling can transcend barriers, build trust, and create common ground. It's time to put these valuable lessons into action. Let's share stories that reflect our shared humanity and the universal desire for a brighter future. Let's connect with, empower, and uplift our African American brothers and sisters, demonstrating the transformative power of conservative principles within their communities. As we press forward, let these narratives be not just a tool for engagement, but a guiding light towards a more prosperous and inclusive future for all.

6

— · —

LONG-TERM ENGAGEMENT: BUILDING TRUST AND INCLUSIVITY THROUGH RECONCILIATION AND UNITY

I n Dallas, as the sun steadily ascended to its zenith, brushing the skyline with a golden hue, James sat in his modest office, suffused with the afternoon light. He was a man in his prime, a quiet force—a leader at the local Baptist church who walked a path steeped in faith and service. His focus today, as it was on most days, lays on the well-being of his congregation and the broader African American community within his neighborhood.

His musings were interrupted by the soft murmur of children playing in the courtyard outside, their laughter a reminder of the youthful potential he was duty-bound to nurture. Thoughts of Proverbs 22:6 echoed through his mind: *Train up a child in the way he should go: and when he is old, he will not depart from it.* This scripture had always been a guiding light in James's commitment to education, inspiring his vision to build a more robust future for his community.

The office was lined with books, their spines promising knowledge and self-empowerment — a small, private library James had collected focusing on entrepreneurship, theology and personal development. He had long embraced the principle that economic independence could uplift his people, learning from the successes and failures experienced in every autobiography. Today, leafing through a book on small business growth strategies, he sought wisdom to support the launch of a local startup incubator nearby.

The phone rang—a local politician on the line, inquiring about James's thoughts on the sanctity of life and his community's pressing needs. As James articulated his desire to see greater personal responsibility among adults as well as stronger nuclear families, his voice was calm yet resonant, as if his spirit was reaching across the line, advocating for those timid to speak their minds honestly in public. *Blessed are the peacemakers*, he recalled from Matthew 5:9, understanding that peace was not simply the absence of conflict between two seemingly opposing parties but also the presence of God in every controversial interaction he has encountered that surpasses all understanding for James.

A knock at the door brought Rachel, a church member and ER nurse, who shared with James a troubling update on healthcare accessibility issues affecting their local community. The conversation unfolded, merging compassion with pragmatism, a patient hopefulness tempering the urgency of their discourse. The mission was clear — advocate for improved care, for Proverbs 31:8 spoke of speaking up for those who cannot speak for themselves.

James acknowledged that the approaching election season would witness a flurry of promises and outreach from politicians eager to court the African American vote. Yet his vision extended far beyond this ephemeral cycle; he yearned for genuine, lasting engagement. How could his church be a catalyst for change, fostering an environment where progress and upward mobility was witnessed across not weeks or months but across multiple generations of its community?

As the day waned and shadows began to fill the room, James sat pondering the strategy that could imbue his endeavors with the longevity they deserved. How might others in positions of influence and power learn to eschew token gestures in favor of sustained, authentic relationships with communities like his own? How might they recognize that true engagement was not merely a political expedient but a sacred duty to love one another as themselves?

From Seeds to Roots: Entrenching a Legacy of Trust and Inclusivity

For the Republican Party to substantively address the residual skepticism often found in many African American voters, an approach that transcends the short-lived fervor of campaign trails is imperative. Trust cannot be rented through periodic here-today-gone-tomorrow attention; it must be earnestly bought with the currency of day-to-day consistency, longstanding commitment and sincere action.

Establishing rapport with African American communities necessitates an investment in daily lives—a commitment to understanding and to advocacy of the people you do life with. To establish sturdy roots of connection that can weather any storm, the Republican Party has to be diligent in how it plants its seeds of engagement and cares for how it stewards its opportunity for growth with a mentality more like a farmer than a hunter.

To foster environments where honest dialogue grows into progress, the lay of the land must first be understood. Cultural, generational and socioeconomic layers intricately weave into the fabric of local African American communities across the country, presenting unique narratives that demand personalized attentiveness. The complexity of building trust predicates a well-versed understanding of the corresponding issues at stake. Policies promoted must subsequently mirror the alignment of Republican principles with the advancement and empowerment of African American communities.

Steps to Sow: Cultivating Community Growth Inclusively

Step 1: Evaluate Local Needs

Allocating time and resources to understand the locally specific challenges that African American communities face is foundational. Quantitative data coupled with qualitative insights gleaned from candid conversations with community leaders and residents provide a well-rounded comprehension of needs. It is from these needs that policy initiatives and improvements should naturally bloom, not from assumed or projected misconceptions.

Step 2: Develop Inclusive Policy Proposals

The proposals crafted should not only answer the call of local needs but do so with the authentic involvement and endorsement of those served. This step is a collaborative dance, one where the Republican Party takes the lead without stepping on the toes of community partners—mutual respect is paramount. We have come to serve, not the other way around. Every policy breathed to life should stand as a testament to the commitment to freedom, self-determination, and the protection and prosperity of all constituents.

Step 3: Communicate the Benefits

Clearly articulate the tangible benefits of policies, demonstrating how initiatives are not temporary band-aids but sustainable fixtures aimed at uplifting individuals, families, organizations and communities. Successes are not to be hoarded but shared, showcasing the replicable triumphs that these policies can yield from one community to another. Speak with passion that resonates with truth and potential, emphasizing how the actions taken are a leap towards shared advancement and individual empowerment within the African American community.

Step 4: Engage in Collaborations and Partnerships

The task at hand demands crossing the aisle of isolation to embrace alliances towards uplifting communities one family at a time. These partnerships among a cohort of schools, businesses, places of worship, and nonprofits, each provide a different thread that strengthens the overall binding promise of inclusive growth and an improved quality of life collectively.

Step 5: Monitor and Evaluate

Ongoing dialogue and sharing among neighbors ensures transparency and accountability. The process mandates that we are simultaneously teachers and students, ready to adapt and evolve based on the feedback received and the sharing of insights and life experiences. Evaluation is not the end but a checkpoint that assesses progress and informs the continual journey forward from which trust and inclusivity can flourish.

Republicans can, through these deliberate and calculated steps, sow the seeds of partnership that grow deep roots within African American communities. Transformative change is built one step at a time.

In order to win over more African American voters, the Republican Party must adopt a sustained presence, genuine engagement, and a commitment to community development. Building trust and inclusivity requires ongoing effort, a commitment to listening, learning, and responding to the needs of the community. This long-term approach represents a significant investment in the well-being and success of African American voters and their families and communities.

The scriptures remind us in Galatians 6:9 that, *"Let us not become weary in doing good, for at the proper time we will reap a harvest if we do not give up."* This passage emphasizes the importance of perseverance and dedication in our endeavors, aligning with the long-term commitment required to foster trust and inclusivity within African American communities.

Remember, this is not just a political endeavor; it is a moral imperative, a calling to bridge divides, and a commitment to the well-being of all members of our society.

7

— · —

AMPLIFYING DIVERSE VOICES: EMPOWERING AFRICAN AMERICAN LEADERS

In the dim light of his modest office, Bernard leaned back in his chair, a silent reflection unspooling in his mind. It was a late afternoon in Washington, D.C., where the hum of the city's pulse resonated faintly through the window. Papers were neatly stacked on the mahogany desk, each an emblem of the ideas he hoped to champion. Ideas that, he knew, could reshape the landscape of political discourse within the Republican Party.

The air was tinged with the crisp scent of autumn, and somewhere nearby, a flag fluttered in the faint breeze, its rhythm steady and determined. Bernard, too, felt the weight of a steadfast resolve, for he saw within himself a vessel of change. He embodied a convergence of heritage and conviction, an African American Republican whose voice carried echoes of overlooked communities, his words the potential to build bridges where divides had long stood for far too long.

As he gazed through the pane, the glinting skyline whispered to him of legacies yet to be forged. Recall chimed within, summoning the guidance from Proverbs, *"Where there is no vision, the people perish."*

There was hardly a more fitting scripture, Bernard reflected, to stir the fiery pursuit of inclusivity and diversity within his party.

Bernard's reverie was broken by the sound of his phone's soft chime, a reminder of the meeting soon to unfold—a gathering of minds where he intended to advocate for the recruitment, equipping, and empowerment of African American Republicans. It was a clarion call that he felt with every fiber of his being, each step taken towards this goal as a testament to his faith and moral courage.

He rose, paced across the room, fingers lightly tracing the spines of books that lined the shelves—testaments to the breadth of discourse that nourished his ideology. His thoughts turned towards the youth he mentored, their dreams and aspirations a hopeful reminder of the future that could be. Their potential, their brilliance, it was all there, waiting to be nurtured, challenged and amplified, to reshape our understanding of what it meant to be a Republican in 2024 and beyond.

Within this temple of reflection and strategy, Bernard prepared to venture forth into the evening's engagement, each stride a muted drumbeat of his conviction. One must equip the dreams of the youth with wings, to soar above the ceiling of their former limitations. And as the door clicked shut behind him, he dared to ponder a question that danced at the edge of tomorrow's promise—how might the pillars of history look upon this stirring of a new generation of leaders?

A New Era of Inclusion Awaits

The strength of a political party lies not just in its policy proposals but also in its ability to empower voices from every corner of the fabric that constitutes the American populace. Nowhere is this principle of empowerment more critical or potentially fruitful than within the African American community, particularly concerning the Republican Party's outreach efforts. As we delve into the ways in which the GOP can harness the unique experiences and perspectives of African American leaders, it is vital to understand that representation matters. Outside of faith in an invisible yet omnipresent God, it's hard to be what you cannot see.

At this juncture in political and social discourse, the importance of diverse leadership is indisputable. When more African American Republicans are entrusted with platforms and responsibilities of influence, such plurality in decision-making and public engagement reflects a powerful commitment to embodying a Republican Party of the people, by the people, for all people. The wisdom from Proverbs 15:22 stands firm: *"Plans fail for lack of counsel, but with many advisers they succeed."* Therefore, integrating a multitude of advisers from various backgrounds is not just wise but essential.

Empowering African American leaders invokes the entrepreneurial spirit, fosters innovation within the party and emboldens others to step up and take action. For the Republican Party, the pathway to empowerment is manifold: mentorship programs, robust platforms for expression, and strategic placement in roles where influence can be exerted effectively. Thus, the party can grow not just in numbers, but in the collective wisdom and experiential wealth that African American leaders can bring in collaboration with other Republican leaders, unified together against a common ideological opposition.

The conversation surrounding diversity of thought within the GOP is not just about inclusivity—it's about enhancing the party's credibility. When a wider range of experiences informs policies and outreach, the fabric of the GOP becomes more resilient and reflective of America's full spectrum. The echoes of Proverbs 27:17 resonate here: *"Iron sharpens iron, so one person sharpens another."* The interaction between diverse perspectives within the party can lead to a sharpening of policy, strategy, mission and vision, ultimately forging a stronger political entity.

When African American Republicans emerge as key influencers, the message to African American voters and the broader community is clear: this is a party that values not just your vote, but your voice. It's about modeling a microcosm of America where every experience adds to the collective wisdom. It's a powerful testament of the GOP's commitment to one united and prosperous nation under God with liberty and justice for all.

Failing to recognize the significance of diverse representation not only undermines the party's appeal to African American voters, but it also perpetuates the misconception that the Republican Party does not value conservatives of different colors and backgrounds. In today's society, where diversity of thought should be championed as much as diversity of our outward differences, the absence of diverse voices can lead to the alienation of potential supporters and limit the scope of the Republican Party's influence amidst a growing liberalism within our nation.

Amplifying Diverse Perspectives

Amplifying the voices of African American Republicans within the party can result in a more comprehensive understanding of the issues facing diverse communities. This understanding can lead to the development of more effective policies and outreach strategies, ultimately strengthening the party's connection with a broader range of voters. When individuals feel valued and recognized for their contributions, they are more likely to be dedicated and engaged members of the party for the long term.

As we understand the impact of amplifying diverse perspectives and experiences within the Republican Party, we must continue to seek opportunities to uplift and value the African American voices that contribute to our party's vision and mission, recognizing that our unity is strengthened through our diversity.

Moving forward, let us commit to actively seeking out and elevating these voices, ensuring that their experiences, ideas, and concerns are integrated into the decision-making processes, policies, and outreach strategies of the party.

8

EXPANDING THE VOTER BASE: ADDRESSING THE NEEDS OF ALL AMERICANS

The soft rustling of leaves outside the window was a gentle accompaniment to Aaliyah's introspection as she sat in quiet contemplation, her study aglow with the afternoon sun. Aaliyah, a community leader and member of the Republican Party, was grappling with a personal quest that seemed to dovetail with her party's imperative for inclusivity. Her eyes, reflecting a myriad of experiences shaped by both triumph and setback, gazed at the portrait of Lincoln on the wall—a solemn reminder of a Republican legacy often distant from the minds and memories of African American voters.

Not far from the window, children walked home from school, their laughter the song of the future—a future Aaliyah wanted to see rooted in diversity and understanding. She realized that stretching out the party's embrace to African American communities was not just about expanding a voter base; it was about proving that conservative values still apply today to sustain human flourishing for all people. She had seen the skepticism first-hand: hard-working families who viewed the party as a distant institution, their needs and priorities a faint echo rather than a resounding chorus. The challenge was to change this perception, to illuminate the principles of opportunity and freedom in a way that resonated with their daily struggles and hopes.

She contemplated the historical - yet often overlooked - stories of success involving African American entrepreneurs, scholars, and professionals who had, against considerable odds, forged paths of remarkable achievement for them and their families before the Civil Rights movement. These narratives, she mused, must be brought to the fore, their truths entwined with policies that supported similar journeys. "Actions speak louder than mere words," she whispered to herself as the pages of her policy review rustled like dry leaves in the wind. Her community programs had to transcend the realm of intention and plant seeds that would flourish in the fertile ground of affirmation and support.

As the day gave way to the purple shades of evening, Aaliyah's phone buzzed; it was time to speak at a local Chamber of Commerce. She rose, practiced and poised, yet a storm of possibilities swirled within her. Her audience tonight would be predominantly African American entrepreneurs—potential change-makers whose trust the Republican party needed to earn. "To serve, to truly serve, one must listen before leading," she would tell them, invoking the spirit of shared enterprise and collective ascent.

So, she set forth, briefcase in one hand and the weight of responsibility in the other, striding with purposeful steps towards the opportunity to bridge two distant worlds. Amid the chattering of dinnerware and the hushed tones of early conversations, Aaliyah imagined the day when the seeds she sowed would grow into a garden where every American could find sustenance — a shared dream of prosperity, community and unity.

What could be done to ensure that this vision for inclusivity and shared dreams was not just a fleeting aspiration but an enduring reality shaping the future of American politics?

Engaging Hearts and Minds for a More Inclusive Tomorrow

The landscape of American politics is ever-evolving, with the tides of public opinion and voter demographics shifting beneath the feet of our nation's parties. It's clear that a potent opportunity lies before us—to broaden the foundations of our electorate by embracing the rich diversity that defines us. At the crux of this strategic expansion is the cultivation of genuine relationships with African American voters, a demographic historically underrepresented within the Republican Party's constituency. This endeavor is not only a matter of political expediency but one of moral imperative and national unity.

As we venture into this dialogue, **we recognize that the African American electorate is not a monolith—within its ranks are a myriad of voices, experiences, and aspirations that enrich our democracy.** Pursuing the engagement and trust of African American voters is tantamount to the Republican Party's commitment to the credence that all are created equal, a principle deeply rooted in spiritual texts and revered as a cornerstone of American ideology. It is by this virtue that we assess the fertile ground for potential growth not just for a party, but for the health of our republic.

The harvest of meaningful outreach is manifold; by more African Americans having seats at the table, breaking bread together with other like-minded and patriotic conservatives of different colors across the country, the Republican Party stands to gain a refreshed perspective on policy, vibrant new voices in its leadership, and a renewed legitimacy in its advocacy for all Americans. By aligning our actions with the biblical principle of "loving thy neighbor as thyself," we engage a strategy that uplifts and empowers, seeking to address the cultural, economic and societal challenges that disproportionately affect African American communities. In truth, the vision of limited government, religious freedom, educational choice, strong family values, safe communities and secure borders, the sanctity of life, and economic prosperity we promote must also reflect the diversity of the nation to truly resonate.

We recognize the symbiotic relationship between an expanded voter base and the potential for positive systemic change. By anchoring our outreach in shared values and intentional actions that elevate the individual, families and community well-being, the party positions itself as a catalyst for positive change.

This strategic pivot mirrors the entrepreneurial spirit, requiring perseverance and an unwavering pursuit of such long-term goals as reconciliation, trust, expansion, and unity, fueled by the wisdom of Judeo-Christian ethics, love for one another and real-world experience.

Expanding the Republican Party's voter base to attract and include more African American voters is a strategic move that can lead to greater representation and a more comprehensive understanding of the diverse needs of the American people. By actively seeking to engage more with the African American community, the party can demonstrate its willingness to listen and address the concerns of a historically marginalized and often overlooked group of people. This not only expands the Republican Party's reach but also positions it as a more inclusive, attentive and unified force within a more balanced and representative political environment, promoting a greater understanding of how conservative values best serve the needs and priorities of all Americans, regardless of the differences God created us all with.

Integrating a broad range of insights from various fields such as theology, politics, and economics further enriches the narrative. By incorporating references and concepts from different disciplines, the Republican Party can create a rich and informative narrative that resonates with a diverse audience. This inclusive approach showcases an understanding of various perspectives, alliances and partnerships that positions the party as an accommodating and enlightened entity.

As we move forward together, let us keep in mind the powerful words, "faith without works is dead." This means that alongside our beliefs and aspirations, we must take actionable steps towards creating a more inclusive, trusting and understanding political landscape. This requires dedication, empathy, and a genuine desire to serve all Americans, regardless of their race or creed. It's a noble endeavor, and one that can propel the Republican Party towards a brighter, more unified future.

9

———

BUILDING TRUST AND RELEVANCE: DISPELLING MISCONCEPTIONS AND ADDRESSING NEEDS

The afternoon sun cast long shadows across the modest community center, where Marcus had devoted much time to fostering a place of unity and growth. Today was no ordinary day, for the reverberations of his latest mission seemed to echo through the very walls of the room, imbued with the gravity of his purpose. Marcus was entrusted with the formidable task of merging conservative principles with the needs and history of the African American community he so dearly championed.

As he arranged chairs for the impending town hall meeting, his thoughts meandered to the delicate bridge he was attempting to construct—a bridge woven from the twine of understanding and the sturdy planks of mutual respect. He recalled the stories of elders, the toils and triumphs of generations, the systemic barriers that still wore down upon the souls of many. Marcus knew the Herculean effort it would take to uproot such deeply entrenched hindrances, to enlighten minds on both sides of the political spectrum, and to articulate a vision where conservative policies could be seen as a key rather than a lock.

The faint hum of traffic whispered in through a cracked window while children played in the distance, their laughter a light note in the symphony of neighborhood life. These were the lives he toiled for, the bright futures he wished to nurture and secure, where potential was not stifled by misunderstanding, doubt or neglect. With every stapled packet of information, every carefully aligned row of chairs, he was setting the stage for dialogue, and, hopefully, for transformation.

Marcus let his gaze fall upon the well-trodden floors, recounting his own journey—a mosaic of faith, of business ventures won and lost, of lessons learned at the feet of mentors and through the grace of trial and error. It was his unwavering belief, drawn from spiritual texts and life's sermons, that through perseverance, faith in God, and the entrepreneurial spirit, every individual within this community held the untapped potential to rise like the proverbial phoenix from the ashes of their challenging circumstances.

The clang of the community center's front door drew his attention, and in came the familiar faces of residents—curious, skeptical, hopeful—all hues of the human spirit seeking a forum for their voices. Red and yellow, black and white, they were all precious in his sight. They greeted Marcus with nods and handshakes, the shared language of a community seeking progress. He set aside his reflections to meet them with the warmth of a host, knowing that tonight, the words spoken and the connections formed could be the seeds of a greater harvest.

As the center filled with the buzz of conversation, Marcus prepared to articulate conservative ideals not as abstractions, but as tangible strategies for empowerment, tailored to the lives and histories of those before him. The room vibrated with energy, anticipation, the sweet tension before the plunge into deep waters of discourse. Could the message he bore bridge the divide, could understanding take root in this fertile ground, could a new chapter of unity and progress be penned tonight, he wondered? Would the community, guided by their faith and united in their resolve, see the dawn of a new day of partnership and promise?

A Path Toward Genuine Connection

The journey to prosperity and societal progress often begins with a single, pivotal step: building trust. For the Republican Party, this means an earnest pursuit to understand and connect with African American voters, crafting a message that resonates deeply within their communities. The first necessary stride is a commitment to proactive engagement. Addressing needs and dismantling misconceptions cannot occur from a distance; it requires a tailored approach, one that involves **walking alongside those you seek to serve**.

Communication serves as the cornerstone for conveying how conservative principles may benefit African American communities. Such dialogue must be rooted in clarity and authenticity to ensure messages don't just reach ears but penetrate hearts. The Republican ethos around self-reliance, family values, and economic independence speaks volumes when connected to practical outcomes and success stories that uplift communities. The Bible holds that *"without a vision, the people perish"* (Proverbs 29:18). The Republican Party's vision must articulate a clear, beneficial future that aligns with African Americans' aspirations and values, infusing a spirit of hope and possibility for better days ahead.

Moreover, the ability to acknowledge systemic barriers and historical injustices is a critical component of trust-building. It demonstrates a reconciliation of past prejudices against one another, repentance of sins committed by previous generations, and a commitment to rectifying inequities to bring us closer together as neighbors, or even better, as reunited brothers and sisters. Not only is this acknowledgment an act of righteousness, but it is also a move toward a future where such barriers are dismantled for all. By applying the principles of Micah 6:8 — to act justly and to love mercy — the Republican Party can extend an olive branch of understanding and collaboration to more of the African American community, setting the stage for genuine restoration and collective advancement to come closer to how our Creator originally intended us to be, before our sins got involved, when living amongst each other peacefully and loving God and one another as ourselves.

Republicans seeking to win over African American voters will do well to remember that in every interaction, in every policy articulated, and every commitment made, they are sowing seeds for a future relationship. The underlying message being: **your wellbeing is tied to my own, and together, we can stride toward a brighter future for the both of us.** This is the art of political engagement that speaks not just to the mind but also to the heart — a path to not only winning votes but also winning hearts towards building a more unified nation.

Communicating how conservative principles can positively impact African American communities is essential to winning over African American voters. It's important to highlight how these principles can directly address the specific needs and challenges faced by African American individuals and communities. By emphasizing the practical, real-world benefits of conservative policies, the Republican Party can effectively engage and connect with African American voters.

First and foremost, **the principles of personal responsibility and self-reliance** are at the core of conservative ideology. These principles resonate with many African American individuals who value hard work, determination, and the desire to succeed against the odds. Highlighting how conservative policies support individual initiative and economic empowerment can demonstrate to African American communities that the Republican Party understands and supports their aspirations for self-improvement and financial prosperity.

Moreover, **economic policies that foster job creation and entrepreneurship** are critical components of conservative principles. By emphasizing these policies, the Republican Party can demonstrate how it aims to create sustainable economic opportunities for African American individuals and communities. Providing examples of how conservative economic principles have directly benefited minority-owned businesses and contributed to job growth within African American communities can effectively illustrate the positive impact of these policies.

Additionally, **a commitment to education reform and school choice** aligns with many African American families' aspirations for their children's academic success. Empowering parents with the ability to choose the best education for their children, whether through charter schools, private schools, or homeschooling, reflects a commitment to educational equity and provides tangible opportunities for improvement in underserved communities. By effectively communicating these conservative principles, the Republican Party can show its dedication to addressing the educational needs of African American families.

Addressing **the criminal justice system and advocating for reforms** that reduce recidivism and support rehabilitation is another crucial aspect. Engaging with African American communities to highlight conservative initiatives that promote fairness in sentencing, offer alternatives to incarceration, and replicate best-in-class re-entry programs to reduce recidivism can bridge the gap between the Republican Party and African American voters. By discussing efforts to address disparities in the criminal justice system and support meaningful reform, the party can demonstrate its commitment to providing second chances for those who have made mistakes, for we have all fallen short of the glory of God (Romans 3:23).

Furthermore, **conservative principles that prioritize family, faith, and community** resonate strongly with many African American individuals. Emphasizing the importance of these values in shaping policies and initiatives can help create a sense of shared purpose and understanding. Highlighting community-based solutions to equip individuals for the real world as responsible and law-abiding citizens, faith-based initiatives to grow communities spiritually, and the significance of strong nuclear family structures to combat the widespread crisis of fatherlessness can illustrate how conservative principles align with the values held dear by African American communities, building trust and relevance.

In summary, communicating how conservative principles can positively impact African American communities involves highlighting policies and initiatives that directly address the specific needs and challenges faced by these communities. By effectively articulating the practical benefits of conservative principles, such as personal responsibility, economic empowerment, educational choice, criminal justice reforms, and support for family, faith, and community, the Republican Party can build bridges and strengthen its relevance with African American voters.

As we continue on this journey, let us also heed the teachings of Mahatma Gandhi, who remarked, *"The best way to find yourself is to lose yourself in the service of others."* It is through selfless service and a commitment to uplifting all members of society that we strengthen the fabric of our communities and build enduring trust.

The path to success lies in our steadfast dedication to dispelling party misconceptions, communicating the benefits of conservatism effectively, and addressing historical injustices towards reconciliation with one another. It is through these actions that we will bridge the gap and forge a stronger, more inclusive future for the Republican Party.

10

— : —

DRIVING POSITIVE CHANGE: THE ROLE OF POLITICALLY ENGAGED INDIVIDUALS

A midst the hushed reverence pervading the library of a subur-
ban home, Michael sat enveloped in a silent struggle. Sunlight
spilled through the expansive bay window, casting prisms of light that
danced across walls laden with texts covering theology, politics, and
economics. A gentle April breeze whispered through the slightly ajar
window, carrying the distant laughter of children at play. But such
serenity felt far from Michael's contemplative stare, fixed on a framed
photograph on his desk – a keepsake from a recent community outreach event he had organized.

In that captured moment, his smile was broad, surrounded by diverse faces, but the unease nested deep in his chest was absent. Today, reality knocked on the door to his conscience with a persistent
question: "How could he, a deeply engaged member of the Republican Party, resonate with fellow African American voters whose trust
seemed like a fortress he had yet to breach?"

He recalled a sermon where his pastor, borrowing from Proverbs
22:1, had preached that "*a good name is to be chosen rather than great
riches, and favor is better than silver or gold.*" The idea had taken root
in Michael's mission, believing that the cultivation of a 'good name'

— one synonymous with integrity and trustworthiness — would be his guiding star.

Fingers drumming rhythmically on mahogany, Michael resolved that mere strategy was not enough. Effective engagement would demand first, an honest kinship that harkened back to the foundational tenets of faith and community shared across cultural lines. He envisioned interfacing with African American churches, sharing not just political viewpoints but participating in discussions on familial and spiritual values.

His interlude with these visions was sliced by the abrupt ting of the phone. The voice on the other end was terse, relaying news about a bill that sought to redress economic disparities in urban areas — a perfect engagement opportunity. As the conversation evolved, Michael responded with a sense of purpose, infused with an entrepreneurial zeal. This was a chance to act, to lay down the groundwork for meaningful dialogue and shared goals.

Later, while arranging a town hall meeting, Michael drafted his speech, threading advice from shared experiences and citing examples mirroring his audience's daily lives. This needed to be more than idealistic rhetoric; it had to spark a tangible change, inspiring those present to envision a more enduring partnership.

Having finished the last sentence, he pondered deeply. Was his approach grounded enough in the shared spiritual principles that often bridged the widest divides? Did his plan resonate with the echo of authenticity required to alter the course of relationships long defined by skepticism?

The house quieted, and dusk crept in, stretching shadow fingers across the now dimly lit room. Reflective, Michael pondered on the lessons of his entrepreneurial ventures—the tenacity, the devotion, the humbling growth. Echoing the narrative of a seasoned mentor, he reminded himself that the challenge ahead required a fusion of faith-based principles with entrepreneurial rigor.

Michael sat back, and as the stars emerged, casting their glow upon the world below, he closed his eyes and allowed himself a moment to envision success — not his own, but of a community uplifted and unified. The room felt a silent witness to his internal dialogue, one where faith and politics met, not as adversaries but as ancient companions walking a path long trodden by leaders before him.

He opened his eyes, a singular resolve etched upon his face. How would he forge this new chapter where strategy blooms from the bedrock of spiritual unity and genuine connections? And more critically, how would it transform the fabric of a nation's political landscape, should his ambitions unfurl into reality?

Uniting for a Common Cause: The Pivotal Role of Engagement

The threads of political engagement and dedicated activism are woven into the very fabric of our nation's history. The Republican Party, in order to win the trust and votes of African American communities, must understand that this involvement must be transformative and principled. **Politically engaged individuals within the party are not just campaigners or strategists; they are bridge-builders and agents of positive change. Their actions, rooted in respect and genuine interest in others, can create pathways for a sweeping realignment in the political loyalty of African American voters.** For this demographic, the betrayals of the past and the oversights of the present demand a future that acknowledges their importance within the American polity.

Herein lies an undeniable truth: to create a lasting impact, Republican advocates must embody the values they espouse. The Republican Party's mission to bridge the gap with African American voters requires that their politically active members emanate authenticity—modeling the virtue of integrity just as Scripture encourages us to *"let your light shine before others, that they may see your good deeds and glorify your Father in heaven"* (Matthew 5:16). The party's foundations, principles, and objectives need to be communicated not just with words, but with actions that resonate with the lived experiences of African American communities.

Politically engaged Republicans must recognize that their honorable quest is not one of conversion, but rather one of alignment, where shared goals can be discovered and nurtured. In building bridges, Republicans should look to the biblical example of Nehemiah, who sought not only to rebuild the walls of Jerusalem but to restore a sense of community and shared purpose among its people. The task at hand is similar in essence: not merely to erect a structure of support, but to foster a sense of belonging and alignment of values.

An important truth to remember is that **authenticity is the cornerstone of effective engagement**. African American voters are keenly aware of when outreach efforts are disingenuous. Authenticity requires a genuine commitment to acting in the best interest of these communities, even when it does not directly align with specific political objectives. Cultivating trust and genuine connections will ultimately yield more sustainable results in engaging and attracting African American voters to the Republican Party.

Politically engaged individuals hold a distinct position akin to civic architects within the Republican Party. Their influence extends beyond the ballot box, reaching into the construction of strategies that encourage an environment where African American voters feel acknowledged, welcomed and represented. With an understanding of historical contexts and current socio-political dynamics, these individuals have the power to design a blueprint that facilitates the joining of hands across political, cultural and racial divides, especially as **many African American conservatives commonly are ridiculed, silenced, or ousted from their own communities because they think, believe, and vote differently than their friends and family.**

To truly galvanize support, understanding the political process is essential. Political literacy initiatives that educate on the history of African American political thought and engagement, the significance of historical policy decisions on the African American communities, and the power of the political process today for rising African American leaders to effect positive change can empower African American voters to make informed choices.

By facilitating town halls, workshops, and informal gatherings, the Republican Party can demystify the political realm, showing how individual involvement directly impacts collective outcomes. Creating informed voters is akin to nurturing informed consumers; both are critical to the success and sustainability of any venture.

In today's digital age, social media, podcasts, and online forums can supplement in-person meetings and help disseminate the Republican Party's narrative and policies in ways that are relatable and accessible to younger African American voters. Like any organization vying for a competitive edge, leveraging technology carries the potential to vastly expand the party's outreach and influence.

Digital platforms provide a space for ongoing conversation and community building, allowing for real-time feedback and participatory engagement. They function similarly to market research tools in business by offering insight into the hearts and minds of a key demographic, enabling tailored strategies that resonate with their core concerns and ideals.

Commitment to the Long Game

The journey toward earning the trust and support of African American voters is not merely a campaign tactic but a sustained commitment to growth and inclusivity. As any entrepreneur knows, short-term gains are outstripped by long-term visions. Therefore, the investment in relationships, policies, and educational initiatives must be viewed not as a sprint but a marathon—a continual effort marked by endurance, adaptability, and resolve.

As the book of Philippians encourages perseverance towards the prize, politically engaged Republicans must fix their eyes on a future where African American support is not an anomaly but a cornerstone of the party's demographic composition. This requires steadfast patience and an unwavering focus on policies and practices that consistently align with the community's needs and values.

In shaping the future of the Republican Party and driving positive change within the American political landscape, politically engaged individuals must continue to embrace the strategies outlined in this chapter. By prioritizing inclusivity, trust-building, and genuine engagement, they can effectively attract and engage African American voters, contributing to the party's growth and prosperity.

Drawing from timeless wisdom, it is evident that the pivotal role of politically engaged individuals in aligning with the values and concerns of African American voters can be compared to the concept of sowing seeds. Just as a farmer diligently sows seeds, nurtures the soil, and patiently tends to the crops, politically engaged individuals must invest time, effort, and authenticity in building relationships with African American communities. As it is written in the Galatians 6:9, *"Let us not become weary in doing good, for at the proper time we will reap a harvest if we do not give up."*

The journey towards winning over African American voters may present challenges, yet through unwavering commitment and dedication, committed Republicans can overcome them. By continuing to provide accessible and practical solutions, they will facilitate a transformative shift within the Republican Party.

In closing, **the path forward is clear: engage with humility and understanding, sow the seeds of trust, and nurture relationships with the African American community.** As the renowned philosopher Aristotle once said, *"We are what we repeatedly do. Excellence, then, is not an act, but a habit."* Therefore, let the habits of reconciliation, trust building, and genuine engagement become the bedrock of a new era within the Republican Party, as the next generation of conservatives lead the charge in fostering a stronger, more inclusive political landscape.

As we part ways, it is vital to carry with us the wisdom garnered from our exploration. Each of us has a sphere of influence, whether within our local communities, families, workplaces, or social circles. By embodying the principles of inclusivity, empathy, and understanding, we can become catalysts for change, actively working to dismantle barriers and create spaces of unity and trust with conservatives and political independents within the African American community.

Throughout this enlightening journey, we have delved into the complexities of the Republican Party's relationship with African American voters. We have explored the historical context, the values that resonate, and the systemic barriers that warrant urgent attention. Our pursuit has yielded a rich tapestry of strategies and actionable recommendations, each designed to foster genuine connection and empower meaningful change.

As we stand on the precipice of transformation, let us carry forth the wise counsel embedded in these pages. Let us heed the call to action, embracing the power of authenticity, empathy and inclusivity. In our pursuit to win over African American voters, we must remain steadfast in our commitment to addressing their concerns, amplifying their voices, and cultivating an unshakeable foundation of trust.

It is important to acknowledge that our journey, although replete with insights, remains an ongoing narrative. There is no panacea, no singular solution that can cure the complexities of mistrust, prejudices, inequities, and historical wounds. Therefore, it is imperative that we approach this undertaking with an unwavering resolve, persistent in our quest for unity and understanding.

As we go forth into our mission fields, let us remember that the wisdom gleaned from these pages is not a mere collection of thoughts, but a clarion call for transformation.

"Human progress is neither automatic nor inevitable. Every step toward the goal of justice requires sacrifice, suffering, and struggle; the tireless exertions and passionate concern of dedicated individuals." - Dr. Martin Luther King Jr.

May this book serve as an enduring guide, igniting the flames of change and unity within each of us. Let our actions resonate with the resounding spirit of inclusivity and empathy, propelling us toward a future marked by trust, mutual respect, and harmonious coexistence.

God bless you and let's build some bridges for a better future for us all.

ABOUT THE AUTHOR

What is most important to Philip Blackett and what truly forms his identity is his relationship with his Lord and Savior Jesus Christ. Philip's mission for the rest of his life is to Grow God's People, Grow God's Businesses, and Grow God's Kingdom as a good and faithful steward of all God has entrusted him, while having a positive influence on all who he encounters each day as a Kingdom Man.

Professionally speaking, Philip is passionate about helping entrepreneurs and small business owners grow their dream businesses, while utilizing his skillset in sales, marketing and business development. Previously, Philip served as President of Cemetery Services, Inc., a seven-figure business he bought based in the Greater Boston area. It was "his pleasure" to also serve as a Manager for a Chick-Fil-A restaurant.

At FedEx, Philip previously provided support to several senior Marketing executives (including the current CEO) as a Senior Communications Specialist after working on its Corporate Social Responsibility team. Before FedEx, Philip advised investors on Wall Street in New York City as an Equity Research Analyst for Goldman Sachs, where he helped recommend investments in over 100 publicly traded companies across ten industries.

Regarding his education, Philip graduated from the Southern Baptist Theological Seminary with his Masters of Divinity (M.Div) degree with a concentration in Great Commission Studies. He also earned his MBA from Harvard Business School. In college, Philip graduated from the University of North Carolina at Chapel Hill as a Morehead-Cain Scholar, majoring in Political Science and Economics.

Philip is a Life Member of Alpha Phi Alpha Fraternity, Inc. When he is not actively fulfilling his mission, Philip enjoys reading, watching sports, and raising his twin daughters, Sofia and Elizabeth, with his wife Mayra.

BOOKS BY PHILIP

Disagree without Disrespect: How to Respectfully Debate with Those who Think, Believe and Vote Differently than You

Future-Proof: How to Adopt and Master Artificial Intelligence (A.I.) to Secure Your Job and Career

The Unfair Advantage: How Small Business Owners can Use Artificial Intelligence (A.I.) to Boost Sales, Outsmart the Competition and Grow their Dream Businesses without Breaking the Bank

Jesus over Black: How My Faith Transformed Me into a Conservative within the Black Community

Maverick Lineage: What I Learned about Black Conservatism in America

Bridging the GOP Gap: How the Republican Party can Win Over African American Voters with Inclusivity and Trust without Compromising Values

— · —

CONNECT WITH PHILIP

f

facebook.com/PhilipBlackettFB

🐦

twitter.com/PhilipBlackett

in

linkedin.com/in/philipblackett

◎

instagram.com/philipblackett

▶

youtube.com/@PhilipBlackett

♪

tiktok.com/@pblackett

Facebook:

https://www.facebook.com/PhilipBlackettFB

X (Twitter):

https://twitter.com/PhilipBlackett

LinkedIn:

https://www.linkedin.com/in/philipblackett

Instagram:

https://instagram.com/philipblackett

YouTube:

https://www.youtube.com/@PhilipBlackett

TikTok:

https://www.tiktok.com/@pblackett

Blog:

https://www.PhilipBlackett.com